Little Mitchie

HUMMINGBIRDS THAT FLY LIKE HELICOPTERS

TINY BUT MIGHTY!

TRACY VONDER BRINK

CREATING YOUNG NONFICTION READERS

Little Mitchie books spark curiosity and support early nonfiction reading for students in Grades 2-3. Designed to build vocabulary, support second language learners, and prepare readers for middle-grade content, each book includes helpful tips for parents and educators to build confidence and deepen understanding of the world.

TIPS FOR READING NONFICTION WITH BEGINNING READERS

Talk about Nonfiction

Begin by explaining that nonfiction books give us information that is true. The book will be organized around a specific topic or idea, and we may learn new facts through reading.

Look at the Parts

Most nonfiction books have helpful features. Our *Little Mitchie* titles include color photographs and graphic aids, a table of contents, a glossary, and an index. Share the purpose of these features with your reader.

Color Photos and Graphic Aids

A lot of information can be found by "reading" photos, charts, maps, and other graphic aids found within nonfiction texts. Help your reader learn more about the different ways information can be displayed.

Table of Contents

Located at the front of the book, this list shows the big ideas within the text and the page numbers where they can be found.

Glossary

Located at the back of the book, the glossary defines key words and phrases that are related to the topic. These words and phrases can be found in the text in colored type.

Index

Located at the back of the book, an index is an alphabetical list of topics and the page numbers where they can be found.

With a little help and guidance about reading nonfiction, you can feel good about introducing a young reader to the world of *Little Mitchie* nonfiction books.

Little Mitchie is an imprint of:

Mitchell Lane
PUBLISHERS

2001 SW 31st Avenue
Hallandale, FL 33009
mitchelllanepub.com

First Edition, 2027.

Author: Tracy Vonder Brink
Designer: Jen Bowers
Editor: Tricia Hoffman

Library of Congress Cataloging-in-Publication Data
Title: Hummingbirds That Fly Like Helicopters / by Tracy Vonder Brink

Description: Hallandale, FL : Mitchell Lane Publishers, [2027]

Identifiers:
ISBN 979-8-89260-886-2 (library bound)
ISBN 979-8-89260-989-0 (eBook)

Library of Congress Control Number: 2026936357

PHOTO CREDITS
Shutterstock: cover, p.1 ©2024 Itz Chinmoy, p.5 ©2025 Krumpelman Photography, p.6, 22 ©2023 Wirestock Creators, p.9 ©2024 TMEwen, p.10–11 ©2025 Fiona M. Donnelly, p.11 ©2009 StacieStauffSmith Photos, p.12–13 ©2017 James Bloor Griffiths, p.15, 22 ©2019 Petr Simon, p.16–17 ©2012 Charles Brutlag, p.18, 22 ©2020 Richard Seeley, p.20 ©2016 Glass and Nature, p.21 ©2016 Dmitry Kalinovsky.

TABLE OF CONTENTS

Chapter One

IN THE AIR

Hummingbirds **hover** in front of flowers to sip **nectar**. Their wings almost move too fast to see.

MIGHTY MOMENT
Hummingbirds are some of the world's smallest birds. The bee hummingbird is only two inches (5 cm) long!

To fly, an object's weight must be supported in the air by a **force** that goes up. This force is called **lift**. Hummingbirds are the only birds that hover by making their own lift. How do they do it?

Chapter Two

MADE TO MOVE

Tiny hummingbirds have big flight muscles in their chests. The muscles make up almost one-third of their total body weight. That's twice as much as most other birds. These muscles give them the power to flap fast.

MIGHTY MOMENT

Hummingbirds flap their wings faster than any other bird. Some can flap 80 times per second. The fast wingbeats make a humming sound in the air.

They also move their wings in a different way from other birds. Hummingbirds can **rotate** their wings like a **figure eight**. Most birds can only flap their wings up and down.

MIGHTY MOMENT
Hummingbirds can fly faster than 30 miles (48 km) per hour. That's faster than a car driving through a school zone.

Even hummingbirds' hearts help their wings move fast. Their hearts pump at up to 1,200 beats per minute! That's about 10 times faster than most people's heartbeats.

MIGHTY MOMENT
Hummingbirds need a lot of food. They eat nearly half their body weight in nectar and bugs every day.

Chapter Three

WINGS AT WORK

Hummingbird wings' figure-eight movements push air down, but they push air backward and forward too. That gives them lift when they flap both up and down. Most birds only get lift when they push their wings down.

Having more lift lets hummingbirds hover in place. They can hang in the air and sip from a flower for as long as they want.

MIGHTY MOMENT

Helicopters have rotor blades instead of wings. They don't make a figure eight, but they spin in a way that creates lift on all sides. That lets a helicopter hover like a hummingbird.

Changing the direction of their wings and tails lets hummingbirds move forward. They can also turn from side to side. They can even fly backward and upside down. No other bird can do that!

Chapter Four

HELPFUL HUMMINGBIRDS

Scientists study how hummingbirds fly. They hope understanding what the birds do might help us build better drones and airplanes. These tiny birds could teach us a lot!

A CLOSER LOOK

Hummingbird feathers are made of the same stuff as your hair and fingernails. Their feathers look shiny because light bounces off them.

Flying backward, sideways, and upside down lets hummingbirds move quickly between flowers. It also helps them escape predators.

Bee hummingbirds are only found in Cuba. They weigh less than a dime!

GLOSSARY

figure eight (fig-yur ayt) a movement having the shape of an eight

force (fors) an action that causes, stops, or changes something's movement

hover (huhv-ur) to stay in one place in the air

lift (lift) a force that pushes up

nectar (nek-tur) a sweet liquid from flowers

rotate (roh-tate) to move in a circle around a central point

FURTHER READING

Barnes, Rachael. *Hummingbirds.* Bellwether Media, 2023.

Nelson, Kristen Rajczak. *Hummingbirds.* Gareth Stevens Publishing, 2023.

ON THE INTERNET

Fun Facts about Hummingbirds
https://southwest.audubon.org/conservation/fun-facts-about-hummingbirds
Audubon Southwest shares lots of fun facts about what these amazing little birds can do.

Hummingbird
https://kids.britannica.com/kids/article/hummingbird/353273
Learn about where hummingbirds live, how big they are, and more with Britannica Kids.

INDEX